TEXTILES

Meryl Doney

W

FRANKLIN WATTS
LONDON • NEW YORK • SYDNEY

About this book

In this book we look at the ways in which the making, decorating and wearing of textiles have developed around the world. We begin with the many exciting techniques for decorating fabric. We then discover how to make fabric by using simple plaiting and weaving skills. Finally, we look at some traditional ways in which materials are reused and recycled to make even more beautiful objects.

On the left-hand pages you will find examples of original fabrics, with a map to show where each one comes from. Details of how you can make something using the same techniques of decoration are on the right-hand pages.

Most of the steps are very easy to follow, but where you see this sign ask for help from an adult.

A project to do together

In the isolated rural communities of Europe and North America during the nineteenth century, the art of patchwork and quilting had two important functions. It enabled women to use up scraps of old material to make new fabrics. It was also an important way of keeping in touch with friends and neighbours. At a quilting 'bee', everyone used to gather at someone's house to work together on a large patchwork quilt. It gave the women a chance to meet and talk, and to catch up on local gossip!

On page 29 we suggest a way in which you could renew this old tradition, by getting together with some friends to make a 'community quilt'. The quilt could then be sold to raise funds for a local cause or charity of your choice.

© 1996 Franklin Watts
Text © Meryl Doney 1996
This edition 1998

Franklin Watts
96 Leonard Street
London EC2A 4RH

Franklin Watts Australia
14 Mars Road
Lane Cove
NSW 2066

ISBN: 0 7496 2401 9

Dewey Decimal Classification
Textiles 746

Series editor: Kyla Barber
Editor: Jane Walker
Design: Visual Image
Cover design: Kirstie Billingham
Artwork: Ruth Levy
Photography: Peter Millard

Welsh pillow and mirror work embroidery from Maureen Antoniades. Very special thanks to Myra McDonnell, advisor and textile wizard.

A CIP catalogue record for this book is available from the British Library

Printed in Great Britain

Contents

The world of warp and weft 4
Your own textile-decorating kit

Hand-painted banners — India 6
Make a welcoming toran

Painting on silk — China & Japan 8
Make a window panel

Design by blocks — India & France 10
Make a special waistcoat

Printing through screens — Ethiopia, India & Ireland 12
Print your own advertising bag

Patterns with mud and wax — West Africa, Bangladesh & Indonesia 14
Make a decorated cloth

Tie-dye patterns — India, West Africa & Japan 16
Make a colourful scrunchie

Decorating with appliqué work — Poland & Chile 18
Make a felt purse

Stitches and mirrors — Great Britain & India 20
Make an embroidered hat

Plaited braid — Afghanistan 22
Plait your own belt

Threads and looms — Peru, Finland, Ghana & Afghanistan 24
Weave on your own loom

The art of quilting — Wales & India 26
Make a quilted brooch

Patchwork everybody — USA 28
Make a community quilt

Useful information 30

Glossary 31

Index 32

The world of warp and weft

In prehistoric times, people living in the colder regions of the world needed to protect themselves by making clothes to wear. They used natural materials such as animal skins and fur, woven grass and leaves. Needles were made from bone or thorns, with lengths of grass or animal sinew used as thread. The earliest known fabric is a piece of woven linen which was found wrapped around a body in an Egyptian tomb. It dates back to around 3000 BC.

Woven fabrics were produced from plant fibres such as cotton, flax, jute and hemp. They were also made from animal products like silk from the cocoon of the silkworm and wool from sheep, goats, camels, llamas or their cousins, vicuñas. Human hair may also have been used on occasions. Patchwork and embroidery may have developed from the need to darn new patches on old clothes.

Changing the colour of fibres by treating them with dyes is also an ancient art. Part of a poncho made from dyed fabric decorated by tying has been found in Peru. It was probably made around 200 BC. Batik work, which uses a substance like mud or wax to resist dye and so make the design, may have developed in China as long ago as 1000 BC.

A bewildering variety of textiles and methods of decoration is available to us today. Many of the textiles are manufactured on vast machines, but the principles are still the same as those used to make fabrics by hand. By looking at the beautiful things made in different cultures around the world, we can begin to appreciate the skill and artistry of the people who make and decorate them – and be inspired to create new and beautiful things ourselves.

Your own textile-decorating kit

You do not need many expensive items of equipment to make and decorate fabrics, but it is useful to have an interesting collection of materials to choose from. You might like to collect a boxful of textiles such as old cotton sheets, velvet curtains, lace, leather snippets, embroidery, ribbons and braids. These could come from your own home, charity shops, jumble and car boot sales or from friends and neighbours.

Wash each item before you store it. Always remove buttons, beads and other decorations from clothes that you are throwing out. Keep them in a box with your sewing equipment.

Here is a list of the most useful items that you will need for making and decorating textiles:

scissors • craft knife • pencil • tape measure • ruler • brushes • fabric paint • masking tape • coloured silk and cotton embroidery threads • gold and silver thread • chalk • sewing pins • safety pins • drawing pins • paper • newspaper •

coloured inks • felt pens • staple gun and staples • iron and board • needle and thread • sewing machine • rubber gloves • plastic bowl • cold-water dyes • washing powder • elastic • tracing paper • wool • polyester padding

Some useful stitches

Here are examples of the most common embroidery stitches. You can use several together to build up a design.

running stitch

double running stitch

star stitch

cross stitch

edging stitch

Hand-painted banners

Hand painting on cloth is a very ancient art. It probably developed as a kind of portable wall painting. The example shown below is a backcloth for a travelling theatre from the northern region of India. The cloth is unrolled and hung up before the play, so that it acts as an advertisement. Once the play begins, the actors use the banner as their backcloth. In a country where many people cannot read, this form of advertising is very useful. Most people will recognize the characters in the picture and will know which play to expect.

In several areas of India these magnificent paintings continue to be made in the traditional way. They are painted carefully using an outline that prevents the colours from running into each other. The material for the outline is made from a paste, often rice starch, that will wash away once the painting has been coloured. It creates a distinctive 'outlined' style of painting.

These hand-painted banners are commonly found in Indian homes too. A *toran* (above), with the traditional flags along the bottom, is strung across the doorway of a house to welcome visitors and to bring good luck.

Make a welcoming *toran*

You could write a message on the flags of your *toran*. It could say 'Happy Birthday' or the name of a visitor coming to your home.

You will need: a piece of calico or canvas, 108 x 27 cm • soft black pencil • ruler • glitter fabric paint (in squeezable tube) • plain fabric paints • brush • scissors • drawing pins

108 cm
12 cm
15 cm
8 cm
4 cm
27 cm

1 With pencil, divide up the fabric as shown.

2 Now draw your design to fit the squares and flag shapes.

3 Squeeze fabric paint along the outlines of your design. Leave to dry.

4 Colour in the designs with a brush and fabric paints. Leave an extra white edge around each item so that it stands out. Leave to dry.

5 Cut around the flag shapes and neaten edges. Pin up over your doorway.

Painting on silk

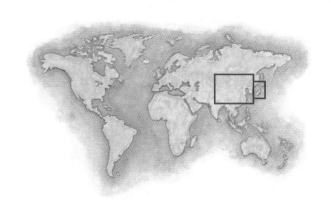

The Far East is famous for the production of silk – a delicate fabric which is woven using thread from the silkworm. The worm winds the fine thread around its cocoon. In ancient times, silk from China and Japan was traded for goods from countries in Europe. In China, a coat made of very fine, transparent silk has been found in a tomb dating back over 1,000 years. Only in recent years, with the help of modern machinery, have we been able to make such fine silk again.

The art of painting on silk developed alongside its weaving. Many famous Chinese and Japanese artists have painted only on silk, and their pictures can be found in museums around the world. This traditional painting (left) has been mounted to form a greeting card, and the modern design (below) has been hand painted onto a scarf .

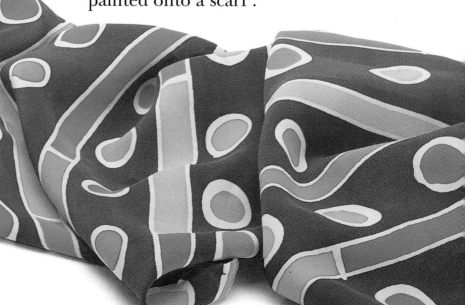

Make a window panel

The thinner the silk, then the more delicate you can make your painting. If you hold your work up to the light it will shine through the silk, just like a stained-glass window.

Practise painting on a small piece of silk first. The fabric absorbs the paint very easily, and thin brush strokes spread out to become fat ones. Use this method of silk painting to make a scarf like the one shown opposite or the window panel.

You will need: plain Habotai silk • scissors • white paper • masking tape • permanent black felt pen • coloured inks • brush • jar of water • old saucer (for diluted inks) • iron and board • small picture frame • staple gun or tacks

2 Use the coloured inks to paint background colours. Paint dark at the bottom and paler towards the top. Dilute your inks with water for the palest colours.

1 Cut a piece of silk a little larger than the frame. Tape the edges to a sheet of white paper. Draw the outline of the fish with the felt pen.

3 Paint the fish using darker colours on the top and paler colours along the belly, to contrast with the background. Leave to dry.

4 Iron carefully. Stretch silk across the back of frame. Secure with a staple gun or tacks. Trim edges. Hang up in the window and see the colours glow.

Design by blocks

Block printing was first invented in India as a way of applying dye to fabric. The process used quite complicated mixtures of dyes and chemicals to make a permanent mark on the fabric. The block designs were carved into pieces of hardwood, and great skill was needed to match each print to the next one in order to form the pattern.

Try curling your hand into a fist and then ink the bottom part around your small finger. Now press the inked part onto a piece of paper. Your fist will make a curled pattern similar to the one shown right. This is said to be how the most traditional Indian design (below right) was formed. In Europe it is now called 'Paisley', after the Scottish town which first copied the shapes from Indian fabric.

Paisley design is still very popular. The finest examples of European block printing, as shown on this head scarf (left), come from France. They are still made by hand, using around 27 different colours printed over each other.

Make a special waistcoat

You can use almost anything to print on fabric: your hand, a shape cut into a potato or a household object like a cotton reel or a sponge. Block printing can also be done on most fabrics, even unusual ones like the velvet used here.

1 Divide lino block into 16 squares as shown. With a pencil, draw this design, or your own design, onto the lino block. With the cutting tool, remove the background areas.

2 Cut fabric in half. Lay one half flat on newspaper, right side up. Brush paint over the raised parts of the lino block. Press the block face down onto the fabric and peel off again.

3 Repaint the block and make the second print next to the first. Repeat until the fabric is covered. Leave to dry. Fix paint by ironing back of fabric.

4 Take your own measurements for A, B, C, D, E, F and G. Draw the simple pattern shown here onto paper, using your measurements. Add 2 cm all around for seams and hems.

5 Pin pattern onto fabric, using printed fabric for the two front pieces and plain for the back. Cut out fabric. Place right sides together and sew shoulders and sides. Hem all edges.

Printing through screens

Screen printing is a relatively modern technique for adding a design to fabric. It was originally developed for printing advertisements and posters on paper. Ink or paint is squeezed through a fine fabric mesh, or screen, onto another surface. Where the holes in the mesh are blocked up, no colour will print. The holes can be blocked using anything from a simple paper shape to a photographically produced stencil. Most of the designs on T-shirts are printed in this way.

These shopping bags were printed in Ethiopia (near left) and India (far left) to advertise the shops which supplied them. The T-shirt is a typical example of a garment that has been printed through a photo screen. It was made to advertise a tour by the Irish rock band U2.

Print your own advertising bag

You will need: a piece of organza, 35 x 40 cm • old picture frame, 25 x 30 cm • staple gun and staples • newspaper • felt pen • craft knife • a piece of calico or thick cotton, 68 x 38 cm • scissors • masking tape • spoon • fabric paints • short ruler • rubber gloves • iron and board • sewing machine or needle and thread

1 To make screen, staple a piece of organza (thin silk) or nylon tights across the back of the frame.

2 To make stencils, trace design twice onto two sheets of newspaper.

Using a craft knife, cut out shape to be printed in yellow on first sheet. Cut out shapes to be printed in red on the second sheet.

3 Cut fabric into one large piece and two strips. Fold large piece in half and lay on newspaper.

4 Lay first stencil on fabric. Mark position of stencil edges with tape. Place screen over stencil and tape in place.

5 Spoon yellow paint onto screen. Wearing rubber gloves, pull ruler across screen, squeezing paint through screen onto stencil and fabric. Peel screen and stencil from fabric. Wash screen. Leave fabric to dry.

6 Repeat with second stencil, using tape as a guide to position. (Don't forget the middle of the letter 'O'). Leave to dry.

7 Iron back of fabric to fix. Turn over top edge of printed fabric and hem. Put right sides together and sew bottom and side seams. For handles, sew fabric strips into tubes. Turn right side out and attach to inside of bag.

Patterns with mud and wax

The technique of dyeing a pattern into a fabric is one of the simplest methods of decoration. The idea is to apply the pattern in a substance that will 'resist', or stop, the dye from colouring those particular threads. When the fabric is finally washed, the resist comes away easily and the pattern is left.

In some countries a starch made from rice or cassava is used as a resist; in others liquid clay or mud is used. The black and white design shown right is an example of Bogolanfini mud cloth. It is made by the Bamana women of Mali, West Africa. The cloth is handspun and painted with river mud.

South-East Asia is especially known for its technique of batik, which uses melted wax as a resist. The wax can be painted directly onto the fabric or drawn on it using a specially made tool called a canting (below centre). The batik scarf (below left) comes from Bangladesh. The pink and white cloth and the leaf-design cloth are examples of batik styles produced in Java and Bali, in Indonesia. The blue material (below) shows how the same technique is used in West Africa.

Make a decorated cloth

We have used an old plastic washing-up bottle to 'dribble' the resist onto the fabric, but you could use an icing bag and nozzle instead. Try out your dribbler on a spare piece of cotton first. Practise controlling the flow and varying the thickness of the paste.

The simple design is based on a square to make it easy to repeat. The deeper the background colour, the clearer the resist pattern will be.

You will need: cotton sheeting (from handkerchief size to a whole sheet) • chalk • tape measure • ready-made starch paste (from art supply shop) • empty washing-up bottle • cold-water fabric dye (dark colour) • plastic bowl • rubber gloves • soap powder • iron and board • sewing pins • sewing machine or needle and thread

2 Fill bottle 'dribbler' with starch paste. Outline each square and add a pattern. Leave to dry.

3 Mix dye in a plastic bowl according to the instructions. (Wear rubber gloves when handling dye.) Put your fabric with starch patterns into the bowl of dye and leave for 20 minutes. Take out and leave to dry again.

4 Wash fabric in soapy water until starch is removed. Dry and iron.

5 Fold in the edges all the way around the fabric and secure with pins. Hem edges and remove pins.

1 Lay fabric flat on a large working surface. Measure out a grid of lines across the fabric and mark with chalk.

Tie-dye patterns

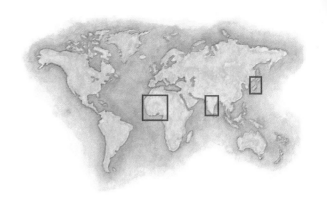

Another method of creating a pattern on cloth is to use threads or knots to prevent the dye from reaching parts of the material. This process is known as tie-dyeing.

Cloth is sewn or tied tightly together and then plunged into dye. When the dyeing process is finished, the ties are undone to reveal the pattern. The small dots on the Indian scarf (far left) are made by tying fabric around the heads of nails fixed in a board.

The strong blue colour of the cloth shown top left comes from indigo dye. It is made by the Dogon and Mossi women of West Africa, who use stitching to resist the colour. Note the difference between the African cloth and the cushion cover (centre left) from Japan. The small, regular dot design on the cushion cover is typical of a simple Japanese tie-dye. The more complicated pattern (near left) has been made using a mixture of stitching and folding.

Make a colourful scrunchie

You will need: a piece of silk or fine cotton, 47 x 17 cm • beads or dried beans • thread • cold-water dye • plastic bowl • rubber gloves • scissors • iron and board • elastic, 12 cm long • needle

Tie-dyeing can be used to decorate many kinds of material. Silk is particularly good because it is very fine and absorbs dye well. When you have decorated your piece of silk, use it to make a scarf, a handkerchief, a wall hanging or the hair scrunchie shown here.

1 Lay a bead on the fabric. Gather the fabric around it, forming a shape like a head and neck. Wind thread tightly around 'neck' and tie. Repeat at intervals until the whole fabric is tied up.

2 Wearing rubber gloves, make up cold-water dye in a plastic bowl. Put your fabric into the dye and leave for 20 minutes.

3 Take out the fabric and rinse. Leave to dry with the beads in place.

4 Cut thread and remove beads. Iron the fabric.

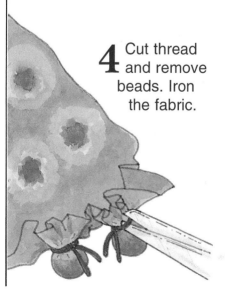

5 Place right sides of fabric together and sew into a tube. Turn the right side out and thread with elastic. Knot elastic in a circle. Sew the ends of the tube together to form a circular hair scrunchie.

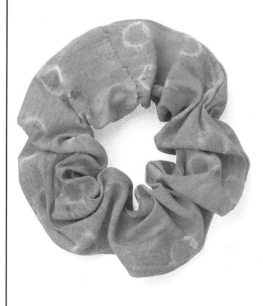

Decorating with appliqué work

A completely different way of decorating fabric is to add colour and texture by sewing or attaching decoration to its surface. The word 'appliqué' means applied, and it describes a method of stitching patches onto fabric. At first this was a way of mending holes in worn clothes, but it soon developed into a method of creating complex and beautiful decorations.

Every culture has its own fabric styles and favourite patterns of appliqué. In cold mountainous regions, felted wool is used for warmth. It is made into coats, rugs and even tents. The felt is often decorated with embroidery and appliqué like this bag from Poland.

In many South American countries the art of appliqué has been extended to include wall hangings. The one from Chile (above) shows scenes of local life. The picture is made by sewing patches of different-coloured fabrics to the surface, using cross stitch. Small doll figures made from fabric and wool have been added to the picture.

Make a felt purse

You will need: one piece of dark-coloured (blue) and one piece of light-coloured (red) felt, 30 x 15 cm each • pencil • tracing paper • scissors • sewing pins • thick cotton embroidery thread • needle and thread

This little purse is made from felt and is decorated with a dog motif that comes from Russia. You could use the appliqué dog motif to decorate a jumper or a birthday gift. You may also like to make a Chilean-style appliqué panel that represents scenes from your neighbourhood, family or school.

1 Fold each piece of felt into three. Cut off the end third of the light-coloured felt.

2 Trace the dog pattern onto the small piece of felt. Cut out.

3 Fold dark-coloured felt into three and place dog motif on front flap. Sew dog onto felt by following the outline with a running stitch (see page 5).

4 Place the light-coloured felt on the back of the appliquéd piece. Pin and tack in position.

Fold single thickness of felt inwards and stitch sides together to form a purse. Remove tacking.

Stitches and mirrors

Embroidery is the art of decorating fabrics using stitching made with coloured threads. Wonderfully detailed pictures and designs can be achieved, but it is slow and painstaking work. In the past, it was considered a fitting occupation for suitable 'gentlewomen and young ladies'. The sampler (right) was made in 1795 by the young Eliza Hall to demonstrate her skill. It is now at the Fitzwilliam Museum in Cambridge, England.

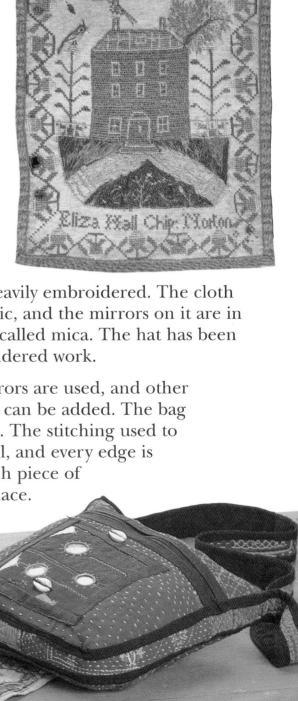

The spectacular embroidery of Gujerat in northern India uses many different stitches, appliqué and small mirrors. Very small pieces of shiny metal are sewn onto the fabric, which is then heavily embroidered. The cloth shown left is a very old piece of fabric, and the mirrors on it are in fact made from a thin, shiny stone called mica. The hat has been made from an old piece of embroidered work.

In more modern times small mirrors are used, and other additions like shells and buttons can be added. The bag below right is a typical example. The stitching used to attach the mirrors is very small, and every edge is covered in thread so that each piece of mirror is held firmly in place.

Make an embroidered hat

The 'mirrors' on this hat are made with mirror foil – a thin plastic that can be stitched quite easily.

You will need: tape measure • pencil • a piece of stiff fabric like linen, about 60 x 40 cm • scissors • iron and board • sewing machine or needle and thread • mirror foil • coloured embroidery thread • buttons • beads

1 Measure your head from front to back and side to side at A and B. Mark measurements on the fabric. Cut out an oval shape.

Measure around your forehead at C. Cut a band of fabric 9 cm wide and C cm long. Fold in half and iron flat.

2 Make up the hat by sewing the top piece to the band on the inside. Sew the ends of the band together.

3 Cut different shapes out of the mirror foil.

4 Sew shapes to band with embroidery thread using edging stitch (see page 5).

5 Sew buttons and beads between mirror patches. Use the stitches shown on page 5 to add extra patterns.

21

Plaited braid

We have been looking at ways to decorate fabrics, but how are fabrics made in the first place? The plaited braid is one of the earliest methods of making fabric, and examples have been found in tombs dating from the Iron Age, which began between 1500 and 1000 BC.

The nomadic peoples of desert areas are always on the move with their animals. They therefore need a method of making fabrics that uses very simple equipment. Plaiting requires only your fingers and no other equipment, so it is an ideal method. The braids or bands are generally made by the men and are used as camel straps to tie down bundles for travelling. They are also used as belts. This decorative camel harness (left) comes from Afghanistan. It has been plaited and decorated with shells and tassels.

The plaiting method is still used today. This nylon towing rope (right) is plaited in exactly the same way as the camel strap, and is very strong.

Plait your own belt

Plaiting seems quite hard to do, but once you have mastered the technique it is very easy. You will see that the plait grows quickly. You can add more colours to change the pattern. You could make a tie, a friendship bracelet or a purse as well as this belt.

You will need: 24 lengths of wool, 12 blue and 12 yellow – 150-cm lengths make a 75-cm belt • length of string • scissors • needle • thread • belt buckle

1 Bunch all the wool strands together and tie a knot in one end. Use string to tie knot to back of chair. Part the strands in half, with 6 blue strands and 6 yellow strands on each side. Work flat on a table.

2 Hold right half of bunch in right hand. With tip of your forefinger go across to left half and pull up alternate threads.

3 When you reach the end of the bunch, grab the last thread and pull it back through the wool to the middle. Add it to the strands.in your right hand.

4 Now hold left-hand bunch in left hand. With left forefinger, pick up every alternate thread in right bunch. Take the last thread through the tunnel of threads back to the middle, and add it to the strands in your left hand.

5 Repeat, keeping the work flat as you plait, until the braid is as long as you need. To finish both ends of the plait, knot each thread to its neighbour to stop the plait unwinding.

6 Cut off excess wool. Turn one end over and sew down. Sew buckle to other end as shown.

Threads and looms

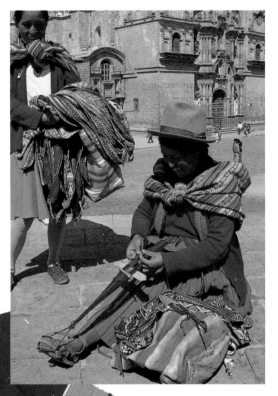

Weaving is a method of joining together two sets of threads by interlacing them at right angles to one another. The set of threads that travels in parallel lines away from the weaver is called the warp. The set of horizontal threads is the weft. Weaving can be done on a very simple kind of loom called a strap loom. The warp is tied to an object and pulled tight, using a strap which is tied around the weaver's waist. This Peruvian woman (left) is using a strap loom to weave cloth.

This type of weaving produces only strips of cloth that can be sewn together to make any size of fabric. The colourful strips below right are examples of the braid still woven in Finland. Each family has its own distinctive design, which is used to identify their belongings. The long strip (left) is an example of *kente* cloth, which is woven by the Asante people of Ghana.

A very good example of weaving and tie-dyeing being used together is in a fabric called ikat. The warp threads are accurately dyed before weaving. The example below is from Afghanistan.

Weave on your own loom

You will need: tape measure • several balls of wool • string • 1-cm dowel, 50 cm long • masking tape • knitting-size safety pin • knitting needle • scissors • darning needle • thread

1 Measure from your chest to your toes. Make a 12-strand skein of wool the same length. Tie a knot in one end and put loop over your big toe.

2 Run the string around your back and tie one end to the dowel. Tape in place. Pass end of wool skein over dowel. Tie free end of string to the other end of the dowel. Arrange wool loops evenly along the dowel.

3 Thread open safety pin from left to right, picking up alternate warp threads. Close pin.

4 Tie end of weft wool to left-hand warp. Lift safety pin and run weft through gap between warp threads. Pull pin towards you to straighten weft.

5 Move safety pin away from you. Thread a knitting needle from right to left, picking up different alternate threads. Lift needle and repeat weaving as before. Do not pull ends of rows too tight.

6 Repeat weaving process (removing and re-weaving the knitting needle each time) until weaving reaches the length required.

7 To finish, pull out dowel and cut warp loops. Using a darning needle sew each thread at one end back into the woven strip. Leave a long fringe at the other end and knot threads in groups of four.

The art of quilting

Quilting was an early way of making clothes and coverings warmer for the winter. In China, beautiful quilted silk coats were made to keep out the cold. They consisted of three layers: a plain backing sheet, a layer of padding and a silk top sheet. These layers were sewn together with tiny running stitches to outline a pattern or picture, or to form a grid of diamonds or squares.

In Britain, a form of plain white quilting using white thread became popular. It is known as 'Welsh quilting' because the people of Wales have developed it into a national art. This silk cushion shows how the stitching forms the pattern.

A quilt style known as *trapunto,* or stuffed work, was developed in Italy. It consists of two layers of fabric which are sewn together with running stitches. Small amounts of stuffing are then inserted through the backing fabric, to make the patterns stand out. The elephant on the Indian bag shown top right is quilted in this way.

Make a quilted brooch

This decorated panel is made out of a shiny gold fabric using a combination of Welsh and *trapunto* quilting. It could be used to decorate a coat or the top of a box. The small one shown here makes an unusual brooch.

You will need: two small pieces of gold lamé fabric • polyester padding • pins • soft black pencil • gold thread • needle • scissors • small gold bead • brooch pin or safety pin

1 Sandwich the padding between the two pieces of gold fabric. Pin down the edges and tack.

2 Draw your design on the fabric with pencil. Sew the outline of the swan (or any animal) in a small back stitch. Use a double thickness of gold thread.

3 Fill in the background with single stitches, like dots.

4 Turn the patch over and cut a small hole in the back behind the swan. Push some extra padding into the body of the swan so that it stands out. Sew up the hole.

5 Fold edges of fabric to the back and secure with running stitches. Sew on a gold bead for the eye. Attach a brooch pin to the back of your panel.

USA

Patchwork everybody

In seventeenth-century England, patchwork quilts became popular as a way of using up snippets of the wonderful fabrics imported from the East Indies. When the early settlers travelled to North America they took their patchwork skills with them.

The tradition has continued until today, and American patchwork, or 'pieced work', quilts (see left) have become famous throughout the world. Many traditional patterns have names like 'log cabin', 'star of hope' and 'Jacob's ladder'.

Families often lived on isolated farms or in small religious communities like the Mennonites and the Amish people. The women used to meet together for quilting 'bees'. Everyone would sew the patchwork pieces together and then gather around a quilting frame to make the running stitches all over the quilt's surface. While they worked the women used to tell stories, swap recipes and catch up on the local news.

Make a community quilt

A community quilt is a fun way to involve your friends and family in making something together. Hopefully the finished product will be a beautiful object that you can either give to someone special or sell to raise money.

Cut several large pieces of plain-coloured fabric into squares and give one to each person. Ask them to decorate the fabric – by embroidering or writing their name, sewing a picture on it or making a hand print. Or you could ask people to supply squares of material from their favourite old clothes.

You will need: lots of same-size patches of fabric prepared by friends (60 squares make a cot-size quilt) • pins • sewing machine • needle • thread • iron and board • an old blanket or length of padding • a backing sheet • length of 4-cm ribbon

1 Lay out your squares so that they form an interesting pattern.

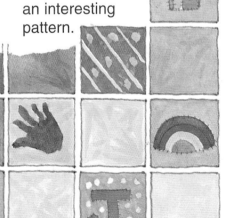

2 Pin the first two squares, right sides together. Sew a 1-cm hem along one side. Press open. Repeat with the next squares to form strips. Pin and sew all the strips together.

(Accurate measurement is important to make sure that the squares lie flat.) Iron squares flat.

3 Make a sandwich of the completed patchwork, padding and backing sheet. Sew along the strips through all three layers.

4 Sew a ribbon around the edges to neaten the quilt.

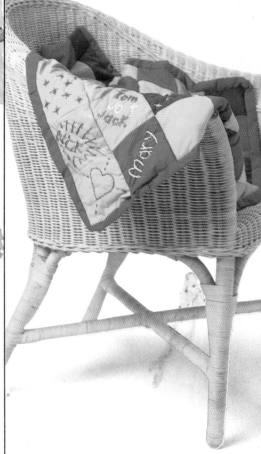

Useful information

United Kingdom

Some helpful addresses

Barnet Multicultural
Study Centre
Barnet Teachers' Centre
451 High Road
Finchley
LONDON N12 0AS

Equipment and materials

The Bead Shop
43 Neal Street
LONDON WC2H 9PJ

CHRISTIAN AID and
TRADECRAFT with
CAFOD & SCIALF
Kingsway
GATESHEAD NE11 0NE
Tyne & Wear

Janet Coles Beads
Perdiswell Cottage
Bilford Road
WORCESTER WR3 8QA
(illustrated mail-order catalogue)

Joliba
47 Colston Road
BRISTOL BS1 5AX
(mail order West African arts and
fabrics)

Naked Zebra
29 Henrietta Street
LONDON WC2
(South African and South
American fabrics)

OXFAM Trading
Murdock Road
BICESTER OX6 7RF
Oxon

Southall Market
Southall
WEST LONDON
(modern and traditional
Indian goods)

Textile Techniques
5 Alexandria Street
RAWTENSTALL BB4 8HP
Lancashire
(information and equipment for
batik)

Museums

The American Museum in Britain
Claverton Manor
Claverton Down
BATH, Avon
Tel. 01225 460503

British Museum
Bloomsbury
LONDON W1
Tel. 0171 636 1555

The Museum of Mankind
6 Burlington Gardens
Piccadilly
LONDON W1
Tel. 0171 437 2224

Museum Quilts Gallery
3rd Floor
254–258 Goswell Road
LONDON EC1V 7EB
Tel. 0171 490 7732

Victoria and Albert Museum
Cromwell Road
LONDON SW7 2RL
Tel. 0171 589 6371

Books

The Art of the Loom
Ann Hecht
(British Museum Publications)

Decorative Beadwork
Debbie Siniska (Letts)

Fabric Art (*Fresh Start* series)
John Lancaster (Watts Books)

Needle Craft
Judy Brittain (Dorling Kindersley)

Textile Arts
Margo Singer and Mary Spyrou
(A. & C. Black)

World Crafts
Jacqueline Herald (OXFAM)

The British Museum Press
publishes a series of books on
textiles from different countries
and regions of the world. It
includes books on the textiles of
Nepal, Indonesia, Thailand,
Africa, Mexico and North Africa.

Australia

NSW:
Craftworld Holdings Pty Ltd
79 Wentworth Avenue
Wentworthville
phone: 02 9896 2390

Victoria:
C & S Craft Materials
51–55 Seymour Street
Ringwood
phone: 039 870 4522

South Australia:
Elde Crafts
76 Main Street, Hahndorf
phone: 08 396 2422

Queensland:
Sundale Handcrafts
16B Loganholme Shopping
Centre
Logan Holme
phone: 07 3801 1121

Western Australia:
Ceramicraft
33 Denning Way, Malaga
phone: 09 249 9266

Northern Territory:
Yee's Hobbies & Crafts
19 Bishop Street
Stuart Park
phone: 089 81 3255

Glossary

Amish A strict religious group found mostly in North America. The Amish separated from a group of Christians called the Mennonites (see below).

appliqué A kind of decoration made by sewing one material on top of another.

batik A technique of decorating fabric by using melted wax to stop dye from reaching some parts of the fabric.

community A group of people who live in one place.

felt Cloth which is made by pressing together wool or other fibres.

fibre A thin strand or thread that makes up a material or fabric.

grid A pattern of lines that are drawn at right angles to each other.

hemp A woody plant with strong fibres. The fibres are used to make rope.

ikat A fabric design that is made by dyeing the threads before weaving them.

indigo A blue dye made from a plant.

jute Fibre from the jute plant. It is used to make items like sacking and mats.

loom A machine for weaving cloth.

Mennonites A Christian religious group whose members have a simple lifestyle and way of worship.

mica A mineral found in the rock granite.

nomadic Describes the lifestyle of travelling people who move around, usually in desert areas, to find pasture and water for their animals.

plaiting Weaving threads across each other to form a piece of material.

poncho A short, cloak-like coat worn in Central and South America.

resist In fabric decoration, a substance that stops dye from reaching the fibres.

tie dye To decorate fabric using threads or knots to stop dye from reaching some parts of the fabric.

transparent See-through.

warp The vertical threads in a piece of weaving.

weaving Joining together two sets of threads, at right angles to each other, to make a piece of cloth.

weft The horizontal threads in a piece of weaving.

Index

advertising bag, screen-printed 13
Afghanistan 22, 24
appliqué 18–19, 31

Bangladesh 14
banner, hand-painted 6–7
batik 4, 14, 31
belt, plaited 23
block printing 10–11
Bogolanfini mud cloth 14
books about textiles 30
brooch, quilted 27

camel harness 22
Chile 18
China 4, 8, 26
community quilt 29
cotton 4

dyes 4, 10, 14, 16

Egypt 4
embroidery 4, 20–21
embroidery stitches 5
Ethiopia 12

felt purse, appliquéd 19
felted wool 18
Finland 24
flax 4
France 10

Ghana 24
Great Britain 20, 26, 28

hand painting on cloth and silk 6–9
hat, embroidered 21
hemp 4, 31

ikat 24, 31
India 6, 10, 12, 16, 20
indigo dye 16, 31
Indonesia 14
Ireland 12
Italy 26

Japan 8, 16
jute 4, 31

kente cloth 24

linen 4
looms 24, 25, 31

mirrors 20, 21
mud, starch and wax patterns 14–15
museum collections 30

natural materials 4
needles 4

Paisley design 10
patchwork 2, 4, 28–29
Peru 4, 24
plaited braid 22–23
plant fibres 4
Poland 18
prehistoric times 4

quilting 26–27
quilting 'bees' 2, 28
quilts, patchwork 2, 28–29

resist 14, 31

sampler 20
screen printing 12–13
scrunchie, tie-dyed 17
silk 4, 8, 9, 17
silk, painting on 8–9
strap loom 24

textile-decorating kit 5
thread 4
toran 6–7
trapunto 26
tie-dyeing 16–17, 24

USA 28

waistcoat, block-printed 11
Wales 26
wall hangings 6, 18
warp and weft 24, 31
weaving 24–25, 31
Welsh quilting 26
West Africa 14, 16
window panel, painted 9
wool 4, 23, 25
woven fabrics 4, 24

Additional photographs:

page 20, Fitzwilliam Museum, University of Cambridge/Bridgeman Art Library, London; page 24 (top), Christopher Rennie/Robert Harding Picture Library.